FAMOUS SHIPS

A Quick History of Ships
with 8 Authentic Models to Make and Display

by Leon Baxter

Ideals Children's Books • Nashville, Tennessee

Contents

Copyright © 1993 by Leon Baxter
All rights reserved.
Published by Ideals Publishing Corporation
Nashville, Tennessee 37214
Printed and bound in the U.S.A.

Created and designed by Treld Bicknell.

ISBN 0-8249-8612-1

Introduction

Throughout history people have been fascinated by the sea and have devised hundreds of ingenious craft with which to journey on its turbulent waters. This book is a short history of navigation told through the stories of eight of the world's most important and exciting ships—ships for trade and ships for war, as well as ships that sailed away to discover new lands.

From the ancient Chinese junk to the powerful *Nautilus*, ships have developed from the wooden-hulled, wind-powered vessels of 4,000 years ago to the super-charged nuclear submarines of today. Eight of the most influential ships are included here in authentic detail for you to cut out, assemble, and sail on imaginary seas.

By following the step-by-step instructions, you will be able to make your own Viking Dragon ship to carry your armies across the water; steer Columbus's flagship, the *Santa Maria*; sail the beautiful *Marco Polo*; fight with the invincible *Dreadnought*; or slip silently beneath the waves in the *Nautilus*.

You will be in control—overseeing production, checking the hull, and trimming the sail. Using the basic hull shapes in this book, you can go on to design and build your own ships for the future, like the sailors and engineers of yesteryear, whose love of ships and the sea inspired the creation of these great vessels. Join the Vikings, the Romans, and the expert navigators of today, and sail away over the seven seas.

Leon Baxter

Construction

Materials

scissors

hobby knife

paper paste or quick-drying glue

paper fasteners

pencil

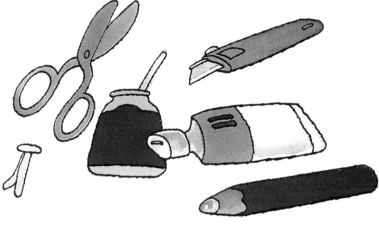

Construction

All of the models in this book are constructed in the same way.

Before you begin, study the picture of the model that you want to make.

Remove the pages from the book by carefully cutting along the dotted lines printed at the inner edge of each model page. When the pages are free, you can assemble each model by following these basic steps:

1. Turn back to these instruction pages and keep them in front of you as you work.

2. Carefully cut out the model parts along the solid black lines.

3. Score and fold along the dotted lines. To score, use the tip of closed scissors to make a light groove along each dotted line—this creates a neater fold.

4. Ask an adult to help you cut along the solid curved lines with a hobby knife.

5. Look at the pictures of the model you want to make and use the pictures as a guide while you glue the ship parts together. Curl the flags, hulls, and sails by pulling them over the edge of your scissors or through your fingers, like this:

6. Roll masts, funnels, gun barrels, flag poles, and the periscope around a pencil before gluing.

7. Carefully cut the mast holes in the hulls and sails like this:

Nautical Terms

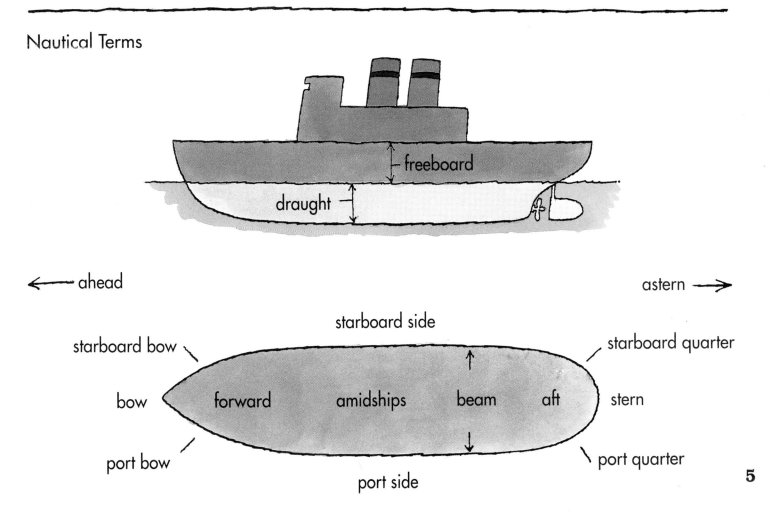

freeboard

draught

←—— ahead

astern —→

starboard side

starboard bow

starboard quarter

bow   forward   amidships   beam   aft   stern

port bow

port quarter

port side

The Chinese Junk

Chinese junks have been in use for over 4,000 years. Their shape came about because the people of ancient China needed a boat that could sail on rivers and canals as well as on the open sea. The Chinese also developed a stern rudder for these boats and used a compass for navigation long before European sailors.

The versatile junk has served as a merchant ship, a warship, and a fishing boat. About 3,000 years ago, giant junks carried a huge variety of trade goods between China, Arabia, and East Africa. The boats were over 300 feet long and could accommodate hundreds of passengers and many tons of cargo. But by the time Marco Polo went to China in the 13th century, the Chinese had lost interest in the rest of the world—and the giant junks sailed the oceans no more.

Junk sails are made of canvas stiffened with bamboo battens, with each batten attached to the mast. The sail size can be adjusted by raising or lowering the sail like a Venetian blind. If a sailing junk sinks, the sail can be rolled up and used as a life raft!

Today, junks are used for fishing and trading along the coast of China—as well as being used as houseboats. But most junks now have engines, and the true sailing junks of yesteryear are slowly disappearing.

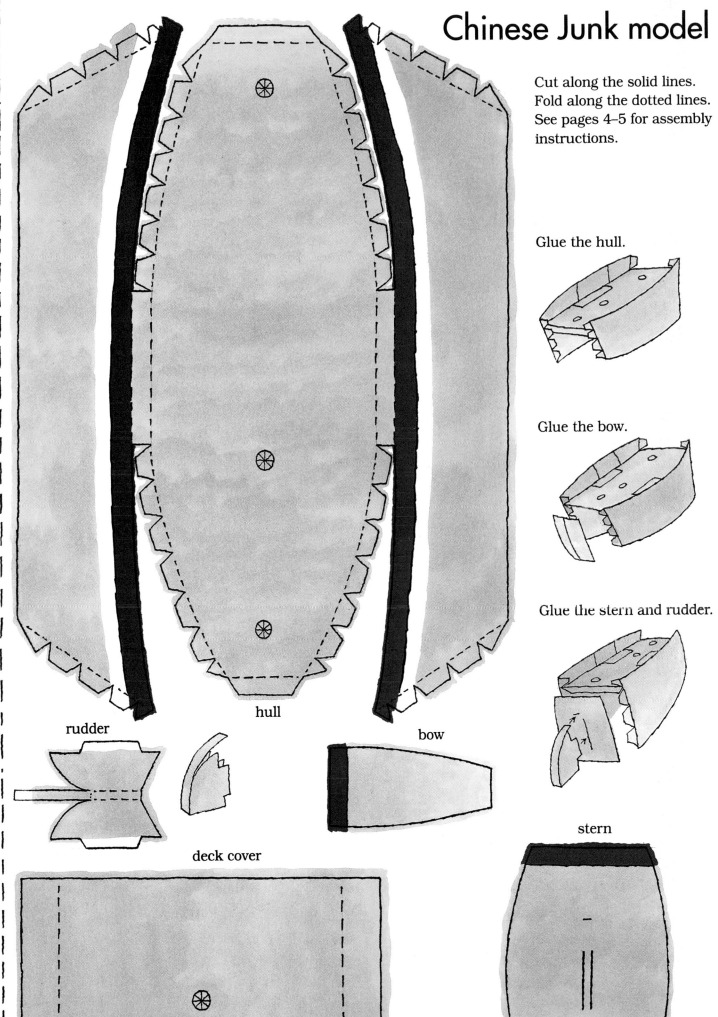

Chinese Junk model

Cut along the solid lines.
Fold along the dotted lines.
See pages 4–5 for assembly
instructions.

Glue the hull.

Glue the bow.

Glue the stern and rudder.

Cut along this dotted line to remove page.

hull

rudder

deck cover

bow

stern

Chinese Junk model—assembly

Cut along the solid lines.
Fold along the dotted lines.

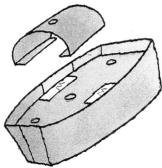

Bend and glue the deck cover.
Line up mainmast holes.

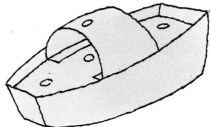

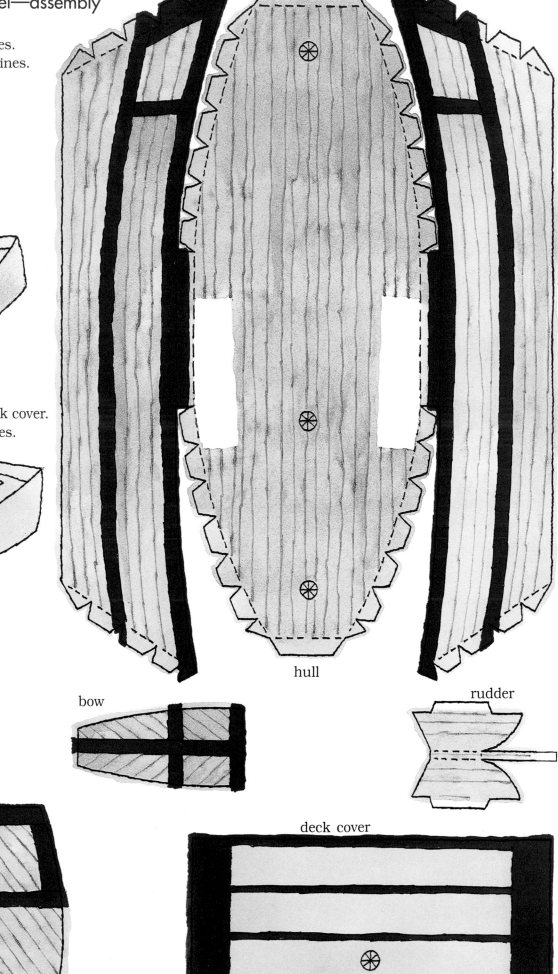

hull

bow

rudder

stern

deck cover

Cut along this dotted line to remove page.

8

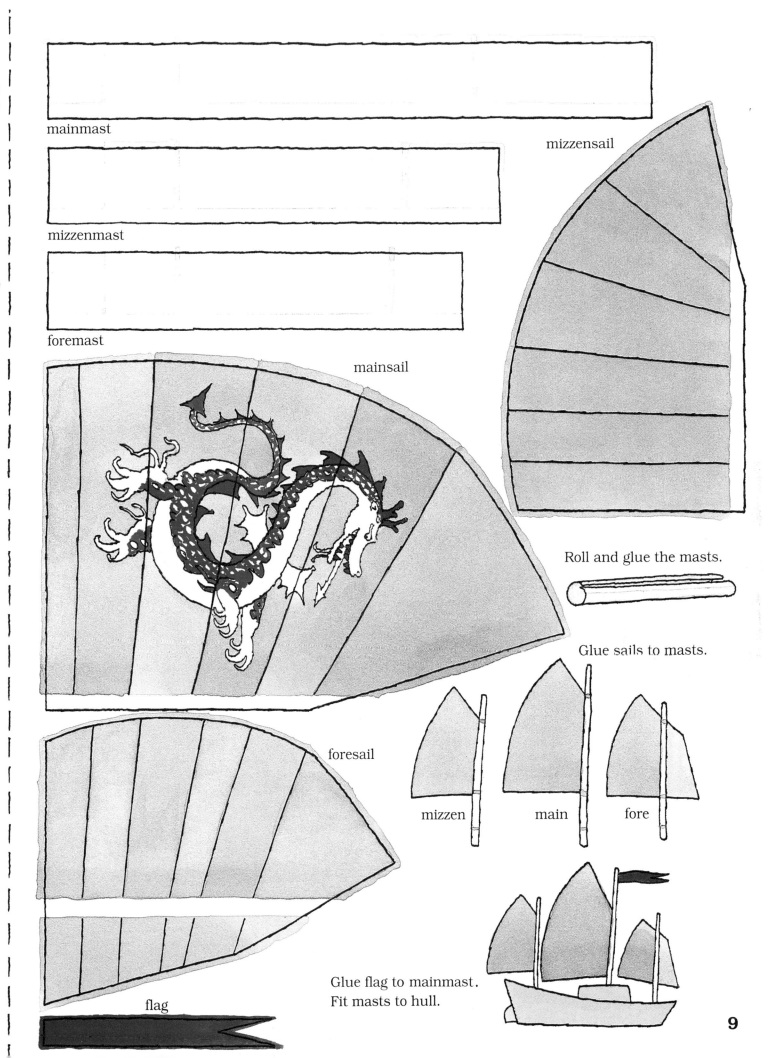

mainmast

mizzenmast

foremast

mizzensail

mainsail

foresail

Roll and glue the masts.

Glue sails to masts.

mizzen   main   fore

flag

Glue flag to mainmast.
Fit masts to hull.

9

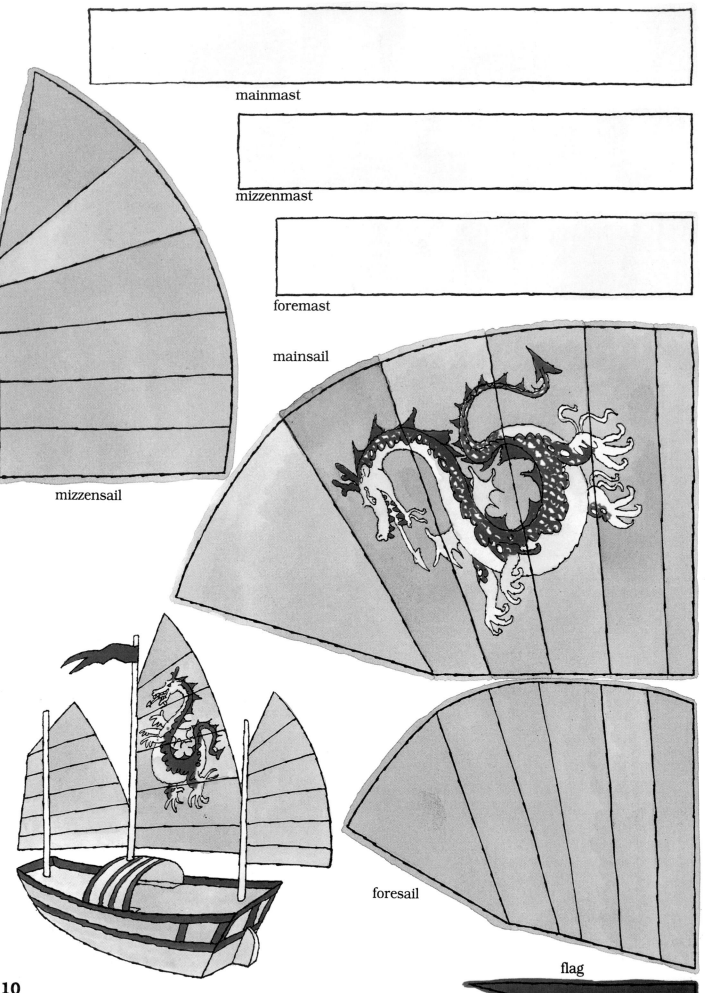

mainmast

mizzenmast

foremast

mainsail

mizzensail

foresail

flag

The Roman Lake

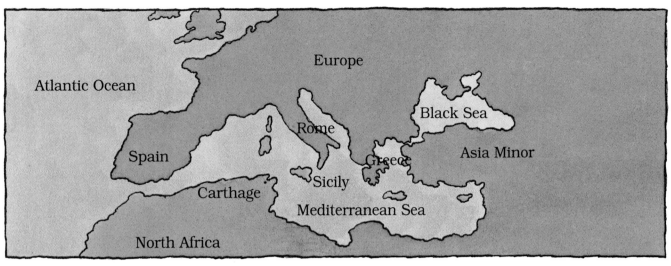

Over 2,000 years ago, the Romans built a mighty empire around the Mediterranean Sea—from Britain to North Africa, from Spain to Asia Minor. They were so successful that, for many years, the Mediterranean was known as "The Roman Lake."

As the empire grew, trade increased and merchant ships brought goods from all parts to the Roman port of Ostia. Wheat came from Sicily, corn from Egypt, and gold and silver from Spain. Olives, dates, saltfish, and timber came from Africa, while jewelry, tapestries, statues, paintings, and furniture came from Greece and Asia Minor. Slaves and wine were brought in from all parts of the empire. Oil and honey were carried in pointed earthenware jars, called *amphorae,* which fitted into specially made holes in the deck of a ship's hold.

Roman merchant ships had two steering oars at the stern, a square mainsail, and a small stunsail at the bow. They were among the first ships to be fitted with a stunsail, which made the ship quicker and easier to handle in light winds.

Although the Romans were not great sailors, they conquered many enemies and gained large fleets of ships. When the wars between Carthage and Rome (the Punic Wars) began in 264BC, the Romans had a battle fleet of Greek triremes, or galley ships with three banks of oars on each side. These vessels were crewed by Greek sailors. The Carthaginians, however, controlled the sea with a fleet of quinqueremes, or galley ships with five banks of oars.

Rome's strength lay in its land forces and its ability to adapt other peoples' ideas. With the help of the Greeks, they built a fleet of quinqueremes, but still

they feared Carthaginian seamanship. So they developed a plan to help win the wars.

The Romans decided to fight at sea as they fought on land. On the bow of each ship, they fitted a gangway with a spike, or crow, on the end. When a Roman ship got close to an enemy ship, the gangway was dropped, and the spike smashed into the enemy ship's deck. The Roman soldiers could then dash across the gangway, and seamanship no longer mattered. The Carthaginians were finally defeated in 202BC, and the city of Carthage utterly destroyed in 146BC.

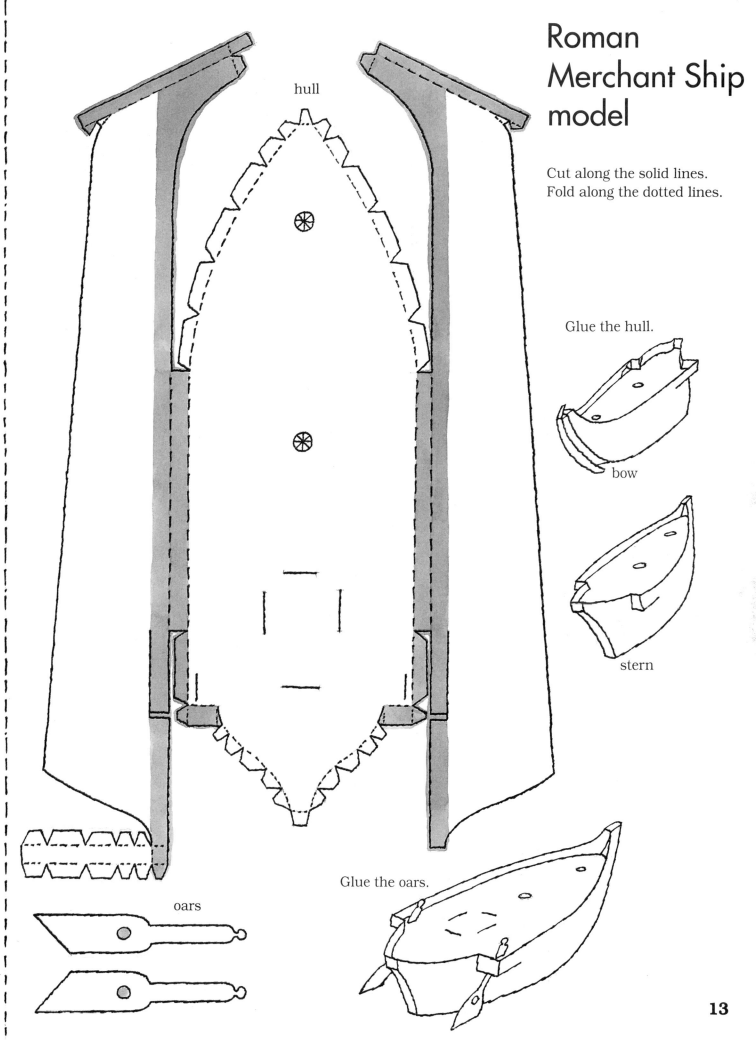

Roman Merchant Ship model

Cut along the solid lines.
Fold along the dotted lines.

hull

Glue the hull.

bow

stern

Glue the oars.

oars

13

Roman Merchant Ship model—assembly

Cut along the solid lines.
Fold along the dotted lines.

Glue the deck cover.
Line up mainmast holes.

Glue the cabin.

Glue cabin to the hull.

hull

oars

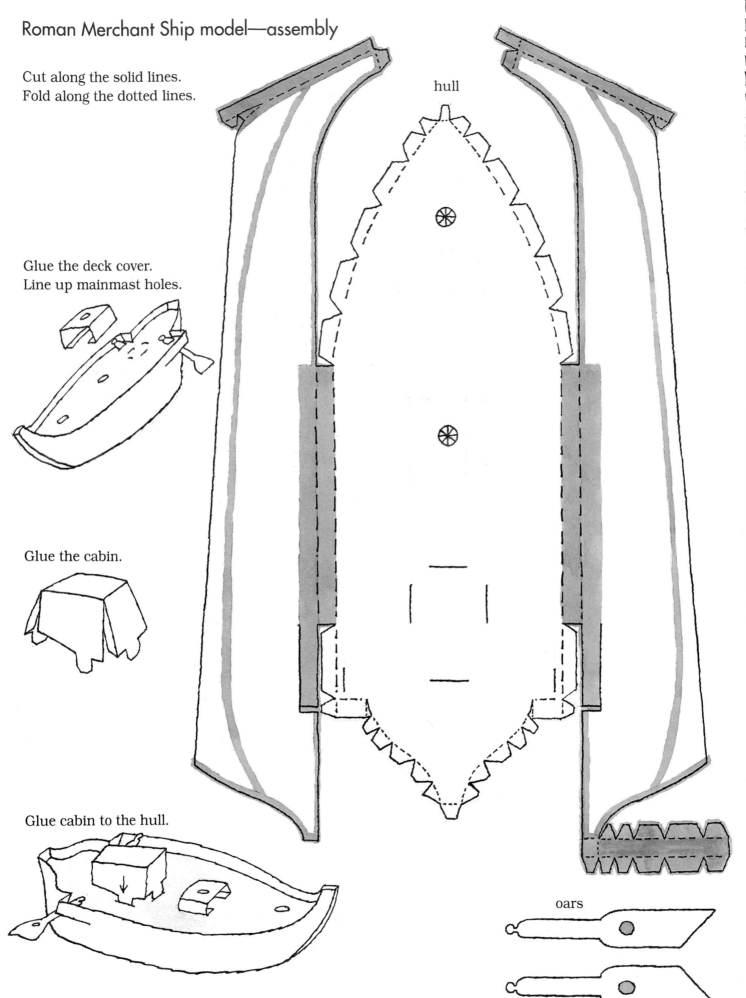

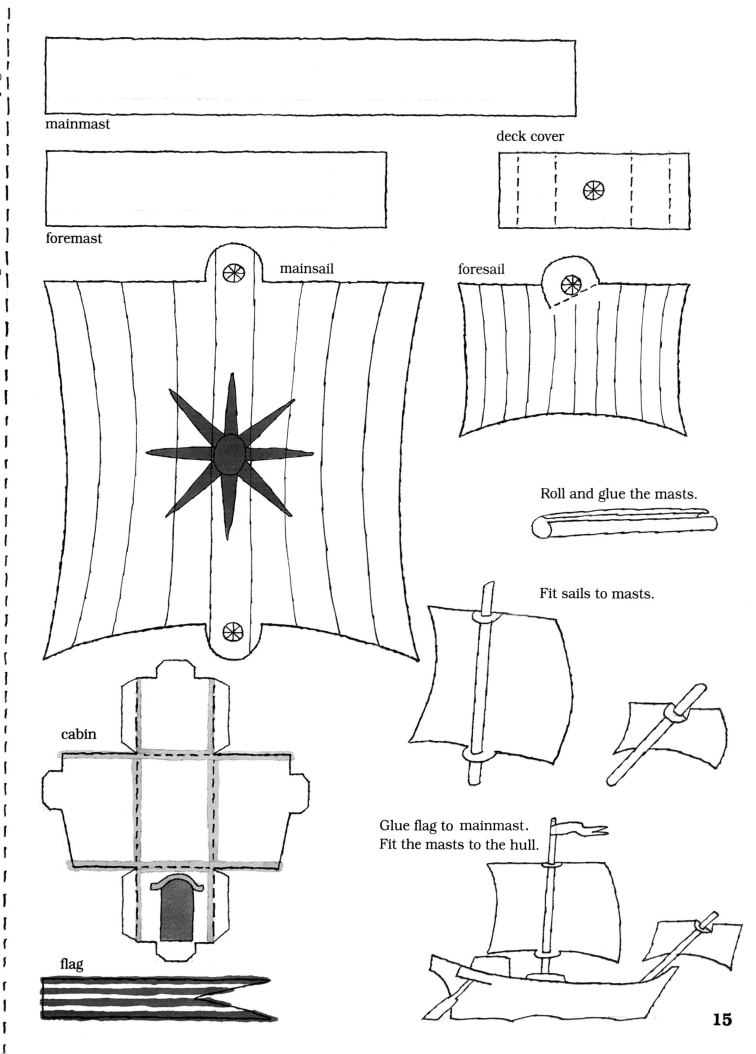

mainmast

deck cover

foremast

mainsail

foresail

Roll and glue the masts.

Fit sails to masts.

cabin

Glue flag to mainmast.
Fit the masts to the hull.

flag

15

Roman Merchant Ship model— assembly

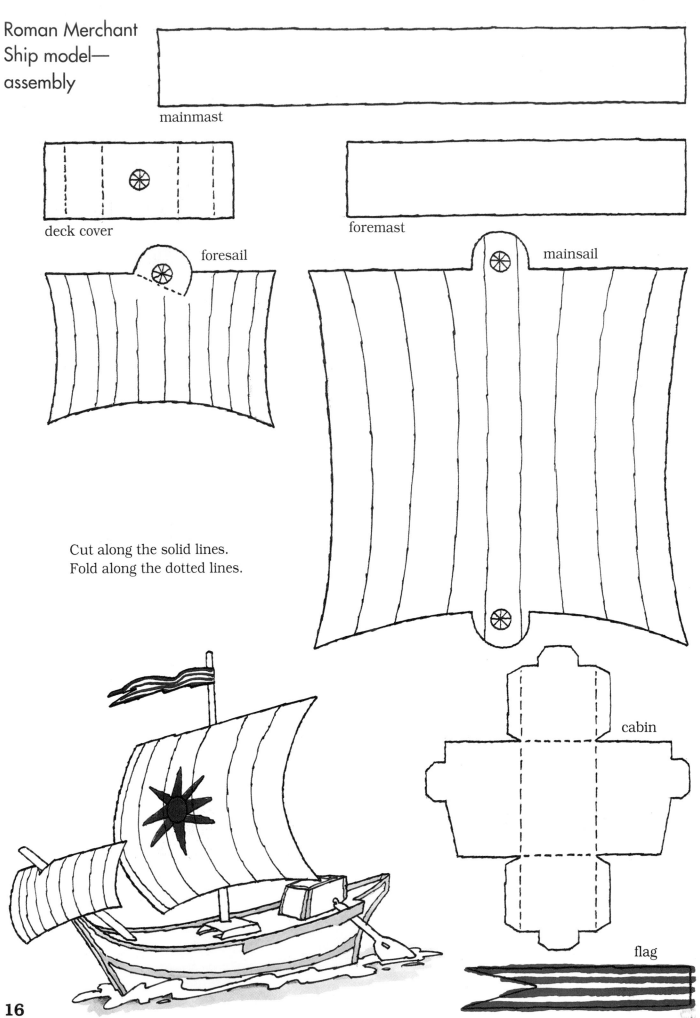

mainmast

deck cover

foremast

foresail

mainsail

Cut along the solid lines.
Fold along the dotted lines.

cabin

flag

Snakes and Dragons

After the Roman Empire collapsed, its lands were attacked by a fierce people called Vikings, who came from Denmark, Norway, and Sweden. They were clever and practical; they used discipline and common sense to win their battles.

The Viking Age lasted from the late 700s to about 1,000AD. While the Vikings began as raiders and pirates, they soon became settlers and traders. Their enterprise, good business sense, and well-designed ships helped them to build a trading empire that spread from Scandinavia to North Africa, and from North America to Russia.

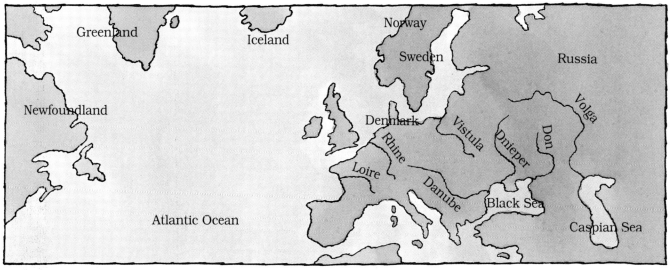

Although the Vikings were expert sailors, they, like the Romans, fought battles at sea as they fought on land. On land they formed a *skaldborg*, or shield fort. At sea they tied their ships together to make a floating fort, and after firing a cloud of arrows, they would board the enemy vessel as quickly as possible. Viking warriors were called *berserkirs*, because in battle they would go "berserk," fighting and slashing in a mad frenzy.

Rules on board a Viking ship were very strict. Each sailor had to swear to be brave and never to speak of fear or to complain. Any shipmate killed was to be avenged, and the worst crime was to betray a friend.

Viking ships were long, narrow, and light. They were made of wood and had both a high bow and stern. A shallow draught allowed them to float in shallow water. One side rudder, like a large oar, steered the ship very well. A single mast was *stepped*, or set, amidships with one square sail—this worked well when the wind was from the stern or side, but worked poorly when sailing into the wind. If the wind failed, the Vikings took to their oars to keep their vessel moving.

Many different types of Viking ships existed. Light, bending "snake" ships with snake-head bows could carry a crew of 40 men over the roughest seas.

Merchant ships were shorter and wider and were used for carrying goods, trading, and exploring. They depended less on rowing and more on sail than "snake" ships.

The largest of all were the famous dragon ships. These were warships with a dragon bow and as many as sixty men rowing—thirty oars on each side.

Skilled navigation and clever ship design allowed the Vikings to cross an ocean or navigate a river far inland. Enemies of the Vikings never knew when or where to expect an attack from these masters of the water.

Viking Dragon Ship model

Cut along the solid lines.
Fold along the dotted lines.
See pages 4–5 for assembly
instructions.

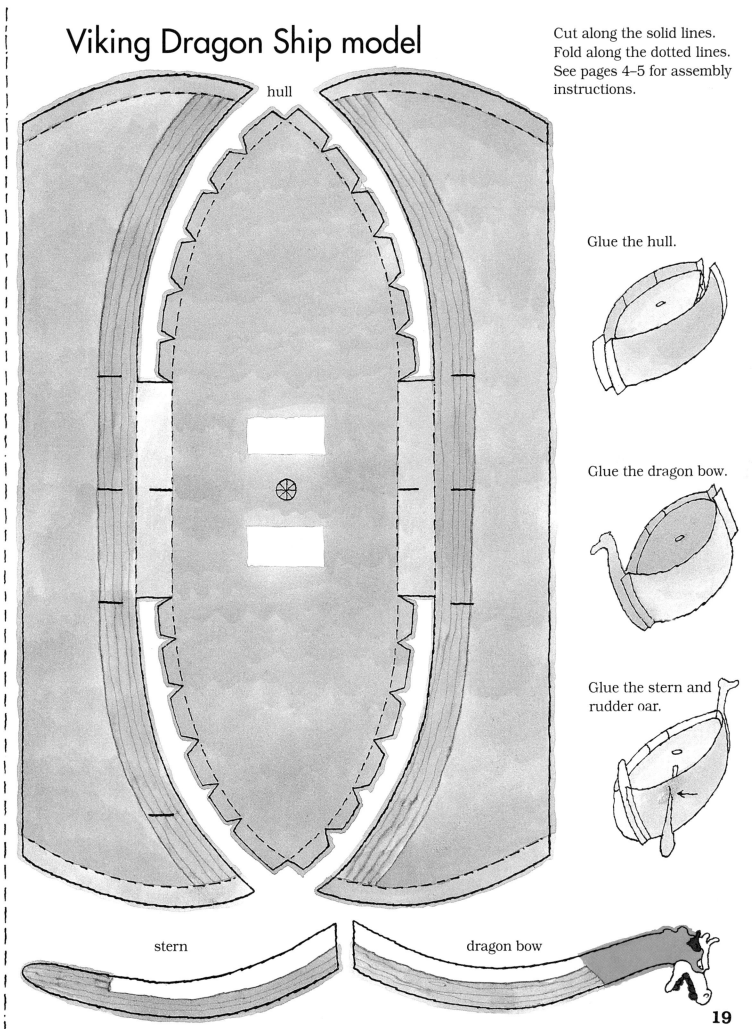

hull

Glue the hull.

Glue the dragon bow.

Glue the stern and
rudder oar.

stern

dragon bow

19

Viking Dragon Ship model—assembly

Cut along the solid lines.
Fold along the dotted lines.

Glue shields to the hull.

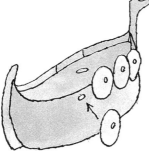

Glue mast support
under the hull.
Line up mast holes.

Fit oars between the
shields.

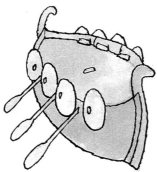

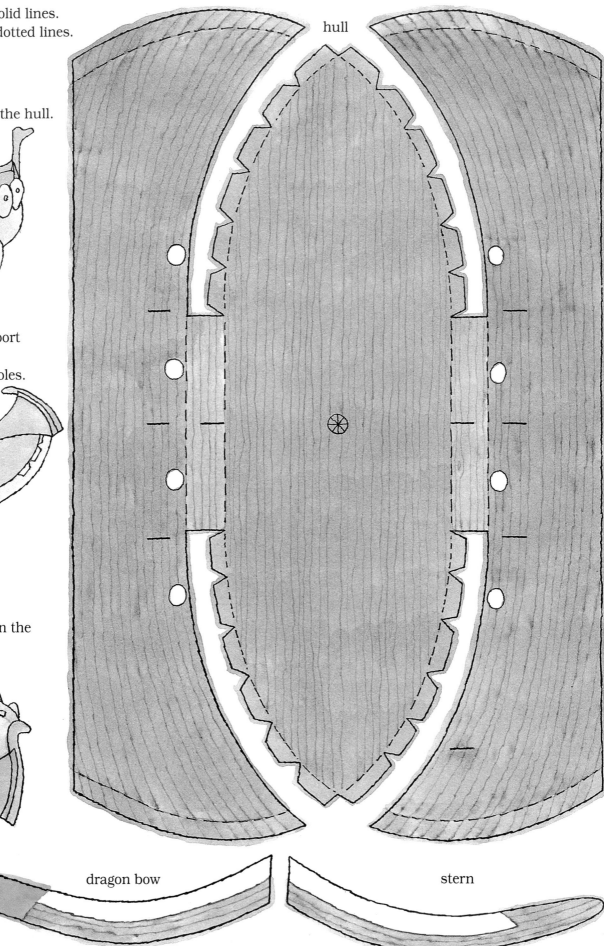

hull

dragon bow

stern

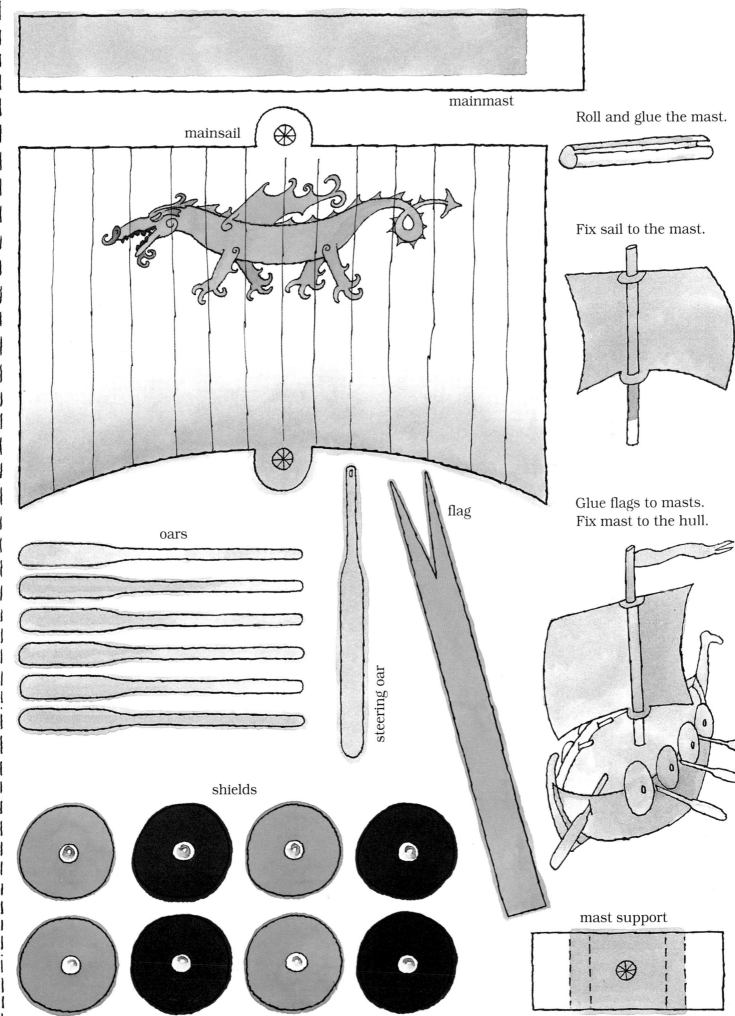

Cut along this dotted line to remove page.

mainmast

mainsail

Roll and glue the mast.

Fix sail to the mast.

flag

Glue flags to masts.
Fix mast to the hull.

oars

steering oar

shields

mast support

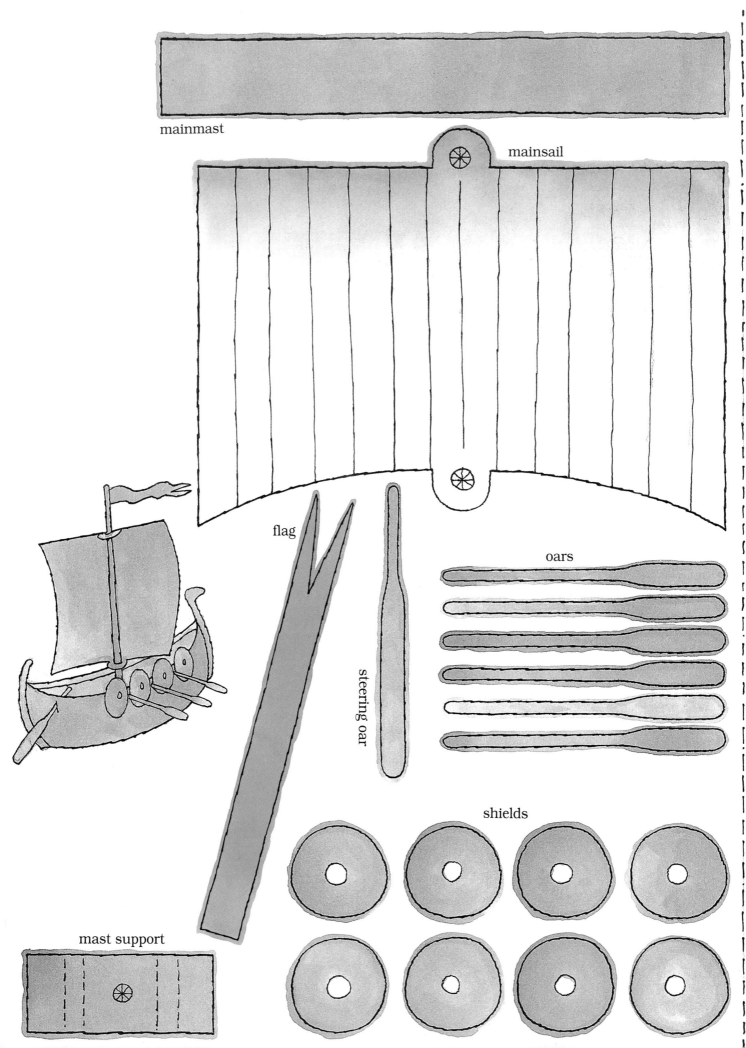

mainmast

mainsail

flag

steering oar

oars

shields

mast support

Cut along this dotted line to remove page.

Christopher Columbus Sails West

"In fourteen hundred and ninety-two, Columbus sailed the ocean blue."

Christopher Columbus was the son of an Italian weaver, but he didn't want to follow in his father's footsteps. Instead he became a sailor, a navigator, an adventurer, and—almost by accident—one of the most famous explorers in history. Like many educated people of his time, Columbus believed that the world was round and reasoned that if he left Spain and sailed west, he would sail around the world until he came to the East Indies, the islands located southeast of Asia.

He set sail on August 3, 1492, but as all the world knows, he arrived in the "New World" of the Americas instead of the Indies.

On the 12th of October, 1492, Columbus landed on the island of Guanahani. The people of the island, later known as Arawak Amerindians, welcomed these strange visitors to their home. Columbus claimed their island for the rulers of Spain and renamed it San Salvador. Sailing on to what he believed to be Japan, Columbus landed first at Cuba and then Haiti, where his flagship, the *Santa Maria,* was wrecked. Leaving some of his sailors behind to form a colony, Columbus returned to Spain to a hero's welcome. He made three more voyages to the New World, but he never did get to the East Indies.

On his first voyage, Columbus had three small wooden ships, the *Niña*, the *Pinta*, and the *Santa Maria*. The *Santa Maria* had a stern rudder, a bowsprit mast with a stunsail and two masts with square sails. She also had a mizzenmast with a *lateen*, or triangular, sail to help her sail "closer to the wind," or toward it.

The two smaller craft were called *caravels*, which also had stern rudders and lateen sails. The fleet was crewed by convicts. It was hard to find men for the voyage because it was expected to fail.

Niña

Pinta

Santa Maria

Since the days of Viking longships, war had changed the needs of sailors. Battles were fought at sea when the crew of one ship boarded an enemy ship; thus ships with high sides had an advantage. Castles—high structures from which the sailors could fire upon their enemies—were now built on the bow and stern. Merchant ships also had castles to help fight off pirates. As was the custom in the 15th century, the *Santa Maria* was built with a high bow and stern.

Cut along this dotted line to remove page.

Santa Maria model

Cut along the solid lines.
Fold along the dotted lines.

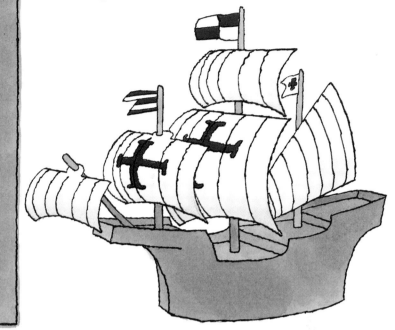

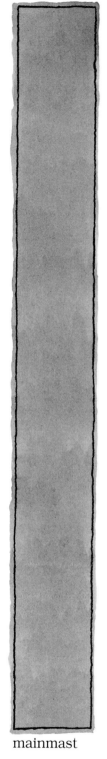

foremast

mizzenmast

mainmast

bowsprit

mainmast support

Santa Maria model—assembly

Cut along the solid lines.
Fold along the dotted lines.
See pages 4–5 for assembly instructions.

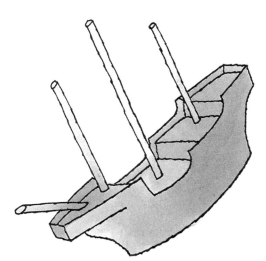

Glue the hull.

Glue mast
support under
hull.
Line up mast holes.

Glue the stern and rudder.

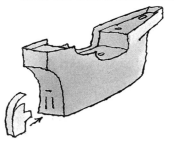

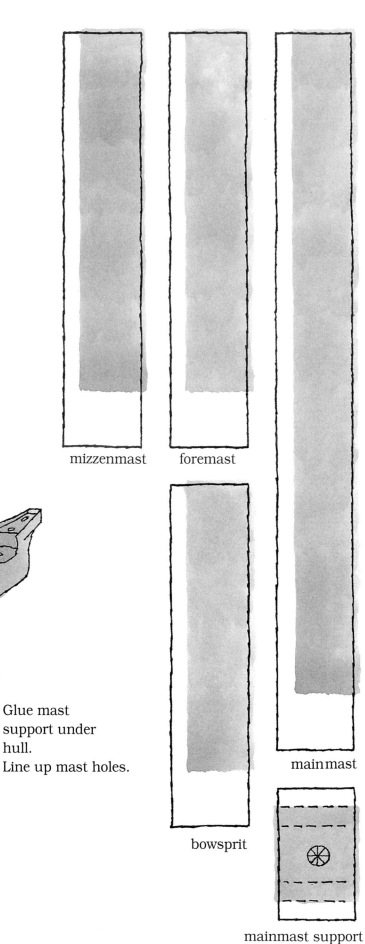

mizzenmast   foremast

mainmast

bowsprit

mainmast support

26

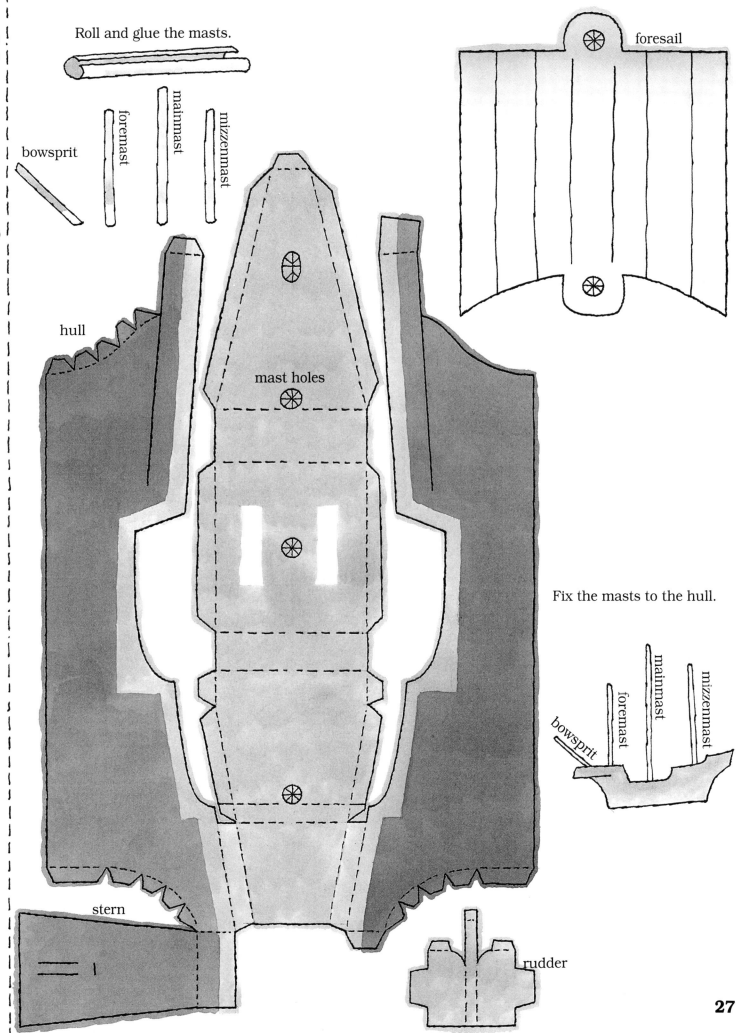

Roll and glue the masts.

bowsprit

foremast

mainmast

mizzenmast

foresail

hull

mast holes

Fix the masts to the hull.

foremast

mainmast

mizzenmast

bowsprit

stern

rudder

27

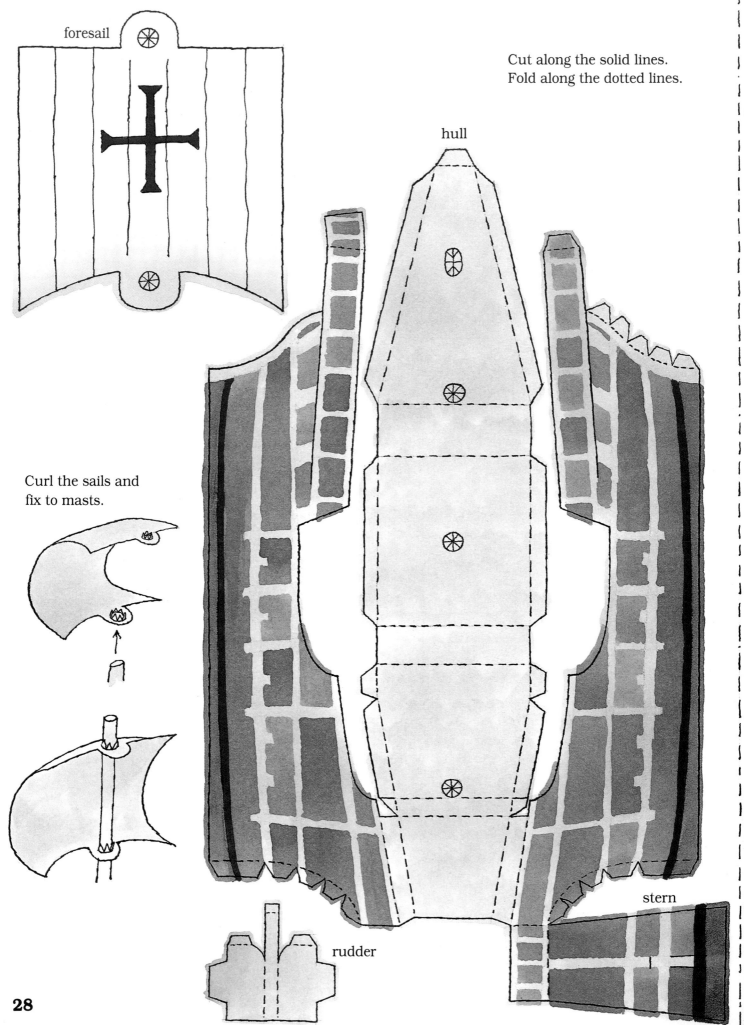

foresail

Cut along the solid lines.
Fold along the dotted lines.

hull

Curl the sails and
fix to masts.

rudder

stern

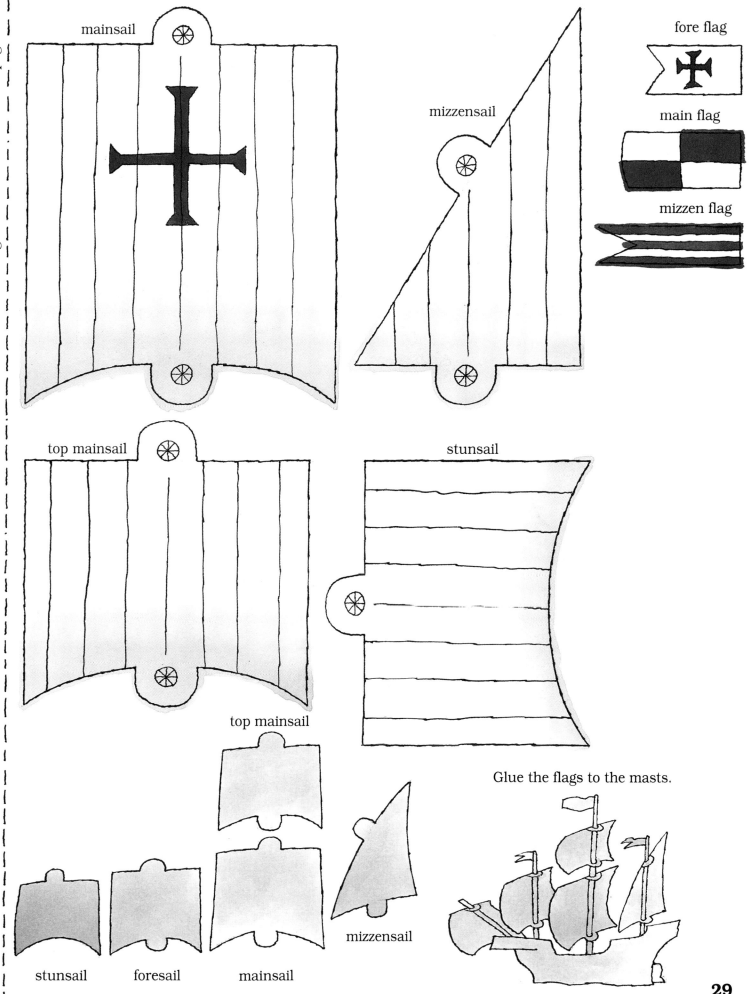

mainsail

fore flag

mizzensail

main flag

mizzen flag

top mainsail

stunsail

top mainsail

Glue the flags to the masts.

stunsail   foresail   mainsail   mizzensail

29

Santa Maria model—assembly

fore flag

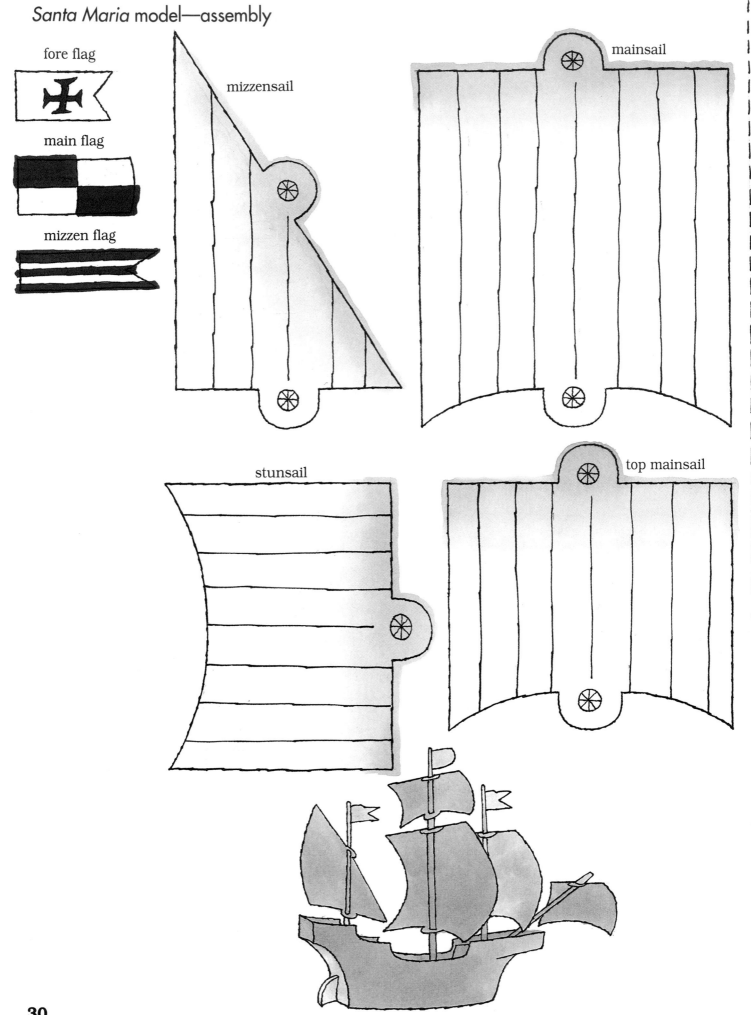

main flag

mizzen flag

mizzensail

mainsail

stunsail

top mainsail

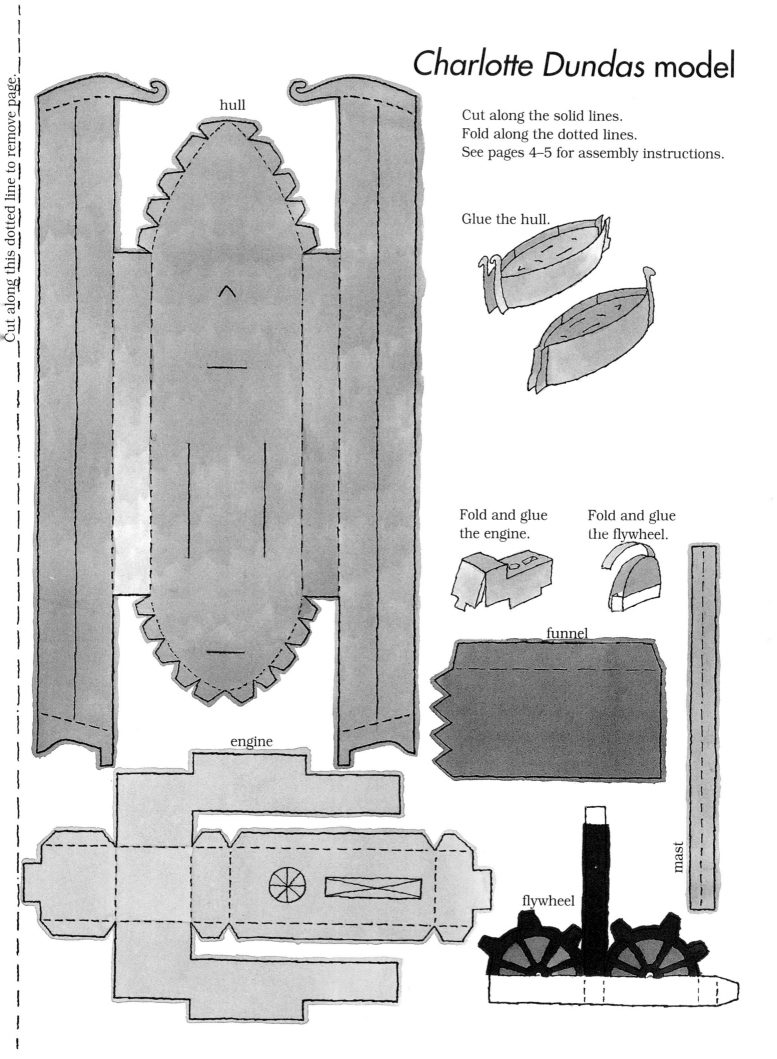

Charlotte Dundas model

hull

Cut along the solid lines.
Fold along the dotted lines.
See pages 4–5 for assembly instructions.

Glue the hull.

Fold and glue the engine.

Fold and glue the flywheel.

funnel

mast

engine

flywheel

Charlotte Dundas model—assembly

Glue the hull.

Fold and glue the engine.
Fit engine to hull.

Fit the flywheel to the engine.

Roll and glue the funnel
and glue to the engine.
Glue the mast to the deck.

mast

funnel

flywheel

hull

engine

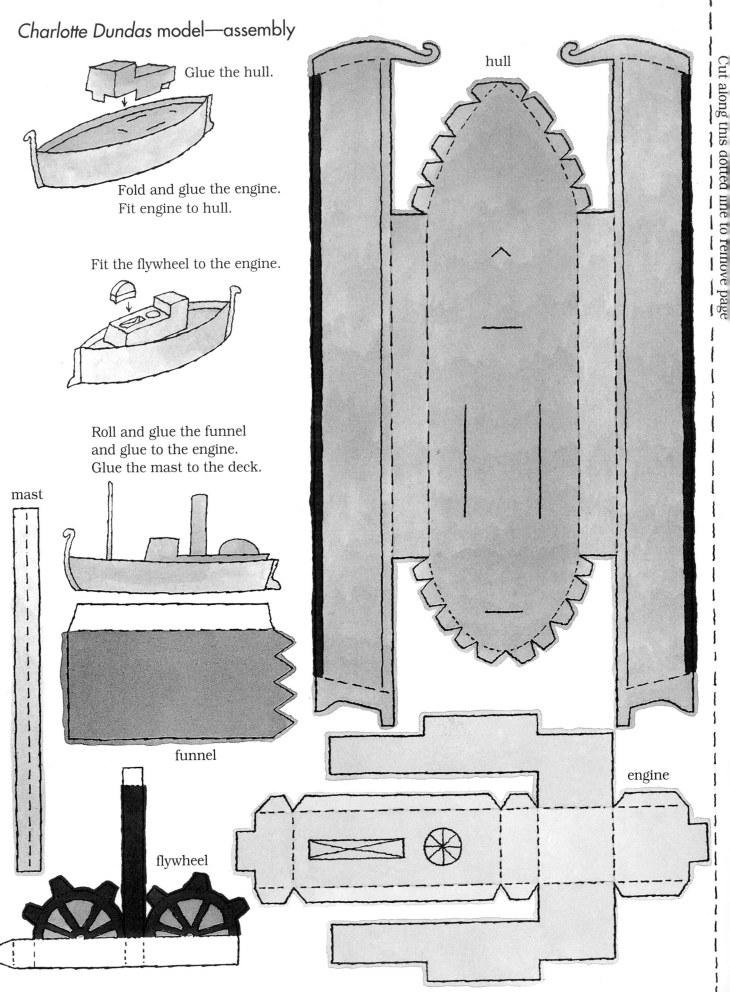

The First Practical Steamboat –
The *Charlotte Dundas*

By the end of the 18th century, people began to think about powering a boat with a steam engine. Experimental steamboats were first built by Patrick Miller in Scotland. In 1801 Lord Dundas, of Scotland, ordered a steam tug from a skilled engineer named William Symington for the Forth and Clyde Canal in Scotland. The tug was launched in 1802 and was named *Charlotte Dundas* after Lord Dundas's daughter.

During her trials—in very bad weather—*Charlotte Dundas* towed two loaded barges 19½ miles in six hours. Lord Dundas was very impressed, but the movement of the tug and barges through the water damaged the banks of the canal. *Charlotte Dundas* was tied up in a lock and forgotten for many years. She deserved better—she was the world's first practical steamboat.

An American engineer named Robert Fulton watched the trials of the *Charlotte Dundas*. Fulton designed and built the first successful steamboat to work in America. His boat, named the *Clermont*, was launched on the Hudson River in 1807. After successful trials, the *Clermont* was given a larger hull and renamed *North River*. She then carried passengers on a regular service between New York and Albany. Very soon, similar steamboats were being built and put into service on other rivers around the world.

Clipper Ships – The Race Between Steam and Sail

Swift sailing ships carried most of the world's trade in the first half of the 19th century, but soon after the first river steamboats appeared, people began to fit steam engines into sea-going sailing ships. The competition between steam and sail began.

In 1819, the American ship *Savannah* became the first steam-assisted vessel to cross the Atlantic Ocean. Later, in 1821, the *Rising Star* left England and sailed around South America and into the Pacific.

As steamships improved, sailing ships tried to compete. They were made longer and stronger, with iron-framed hulls covered with wood. Bows were streamlined with a sharp V-shape. These ships were called "clippers" because they could clip days off the length of a journey. They sailed from America and Britain, making record-breaking round-the-world voyages.

The Canadian clipper *Marco Polo* was known as the fastest ship in the world in 1852. Her captain, "Bully" Forbes, was a man of fiery temper. On one voyage he became angry when he saw a shark swimming alongside his famous ship— and keeping up with his speed! He had the shark caught and brought aboard. The frightened crew watched in horror as the shark crashed through the roof of Forbes's cabin. The captain was sitting inside when the vengeful shark came through his ceiling and smashed his cabin to pieces, but the salty captain escaped unhurt.

Through the 19th century and into the 20th century, steamships improved steadily until it became unprofitable to move cargo in a ship that depended on the fickle wind for power. Sadly, by the 1940s, the stately and beautiful merchant ships no longer raced across the oceans to bring goods to the people of Europe and America.

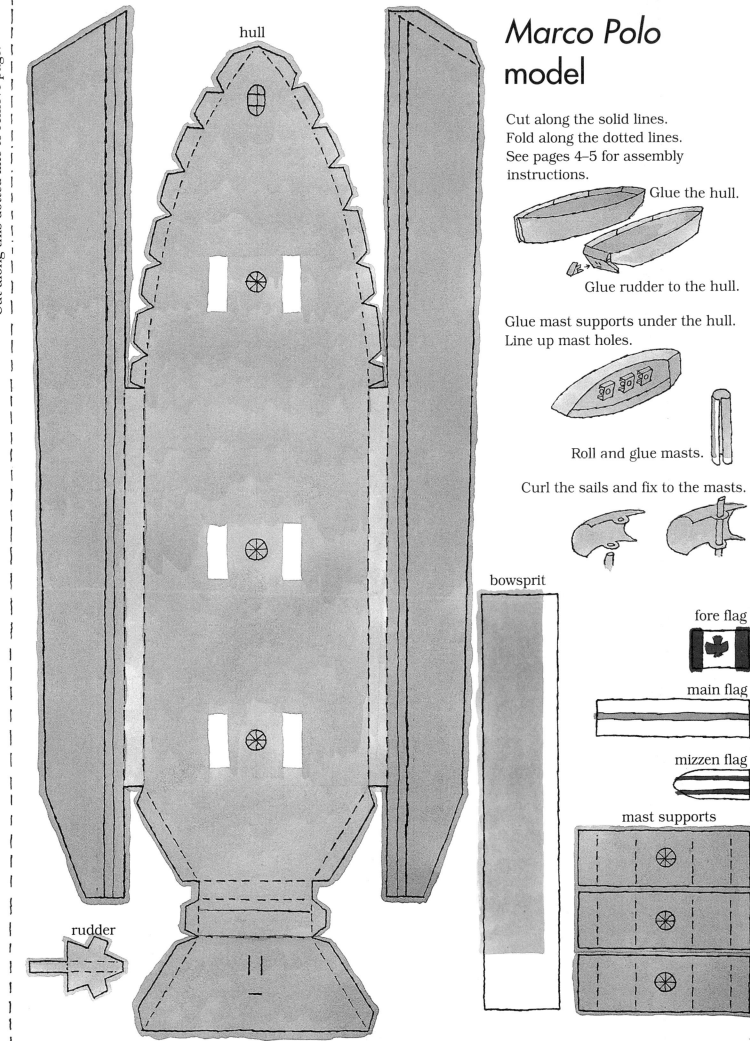

Cut along this dotted line to remove page.

hull

Marco Polo model

Cut along the solid lines.
Fold along the dotted lines.
See pages 4–5 for assembly
instructions.

Glue the hull.

Glue rudder to the hull.

Glue mast supports under the hull.
Line up mast holes.

Roll and glue masts.

Curl the sails and fix to the masts.

bowsprit

fore flag

main flag

mizzen flag

mast supports

rudder

Marco Polo model—assembly

The jib fits like this:

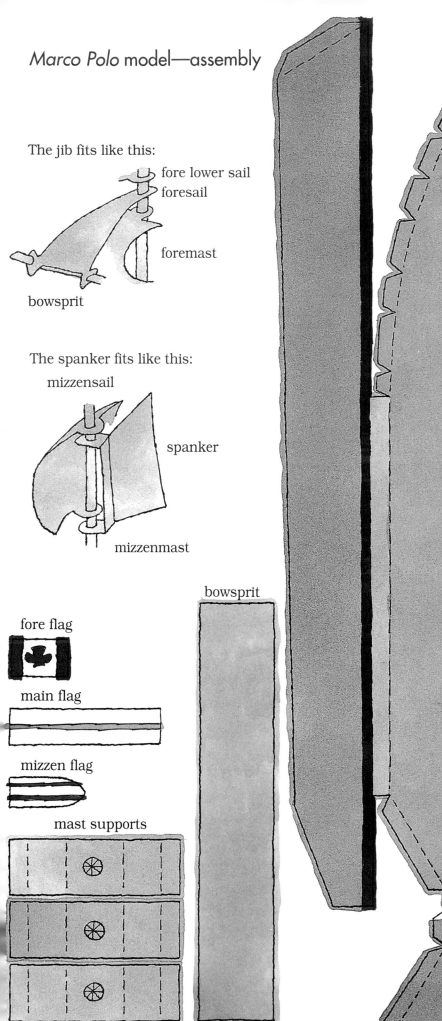

fore lower sail

foresail

foremast

bowsprit

The spanker fits like this:

mizzensail

spanker

mizzenmast

fore flag

main flag

mizzen flag

mast supports

bowsprit

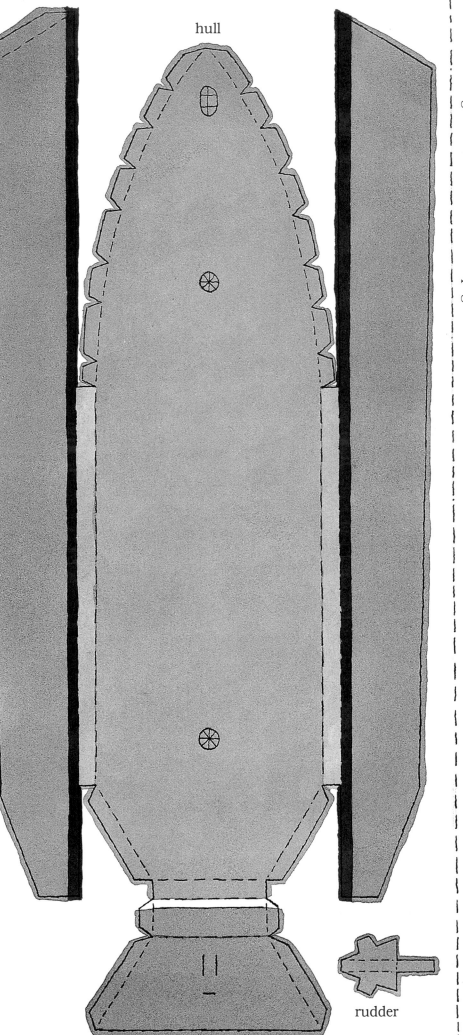

hull

rudder

Cut along this dotted line to remove page.

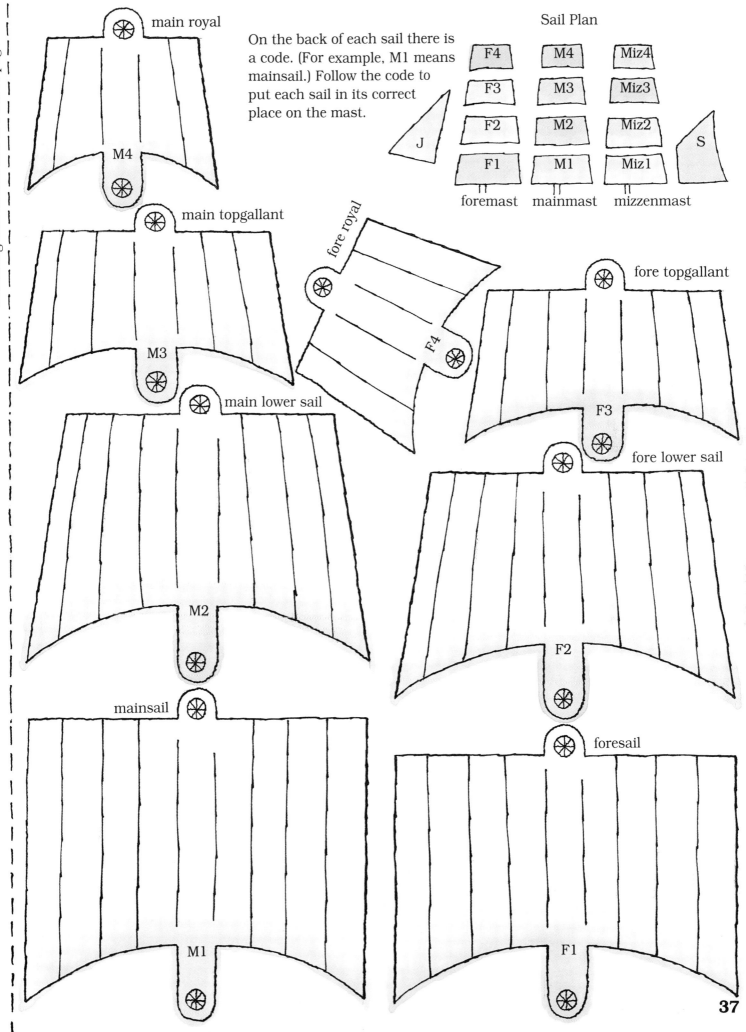

main royal

M4

On the back of each sail there is a code. (For example, M1 means mainsail.) Follow the code to put each sail in its correct place on the mast.

Sail Plan

F4	M4	Miz4
F3	M3	Miz3
F2	M2	Miz2
F1	M1	Miz1

J

S

foremast   mainmast   mizzenmast

main topgallant

M3

fore royal

F4

fore topgallant

F3

main lower sail

M2

fore lower sail

F2

mainsail

M1

foresail

F1

37

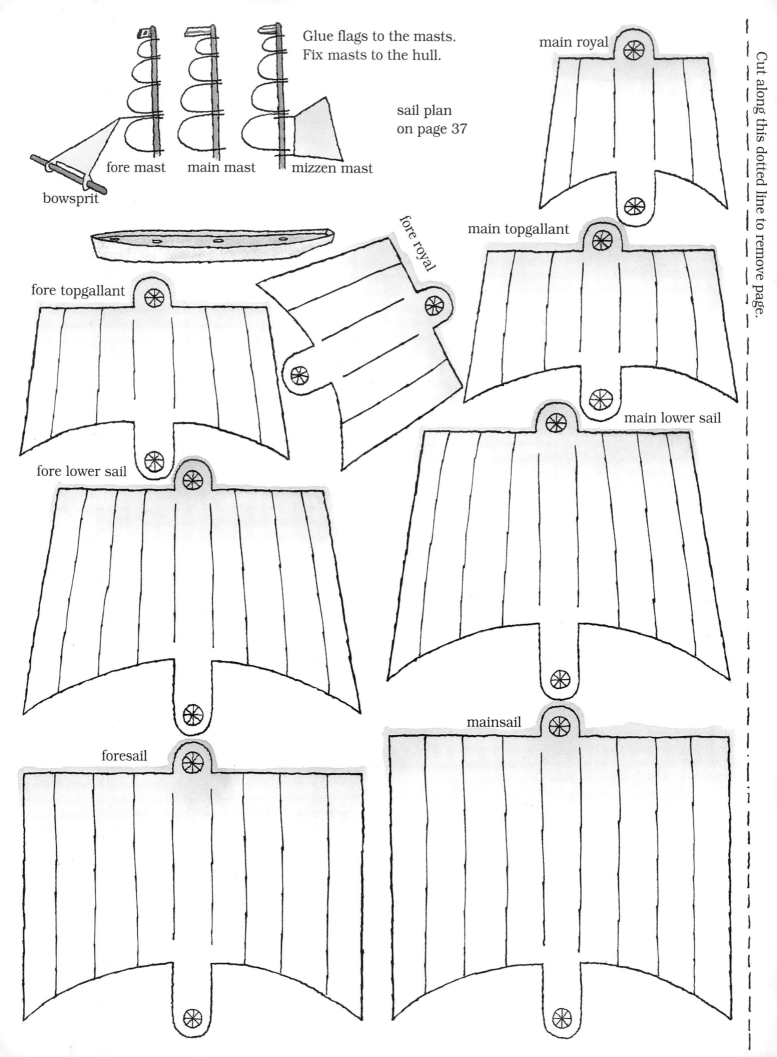

Glue flags to the masts.
Fix masts to the hull.

sail plan
on page 37

fore mast   main mast   mizzen mast

bowsprit

main royal

fore royal

main topgallant

fore topgallant

main lower sail

fore lower sail

mainsail

foresail

Cut along this dotted line to remove page.

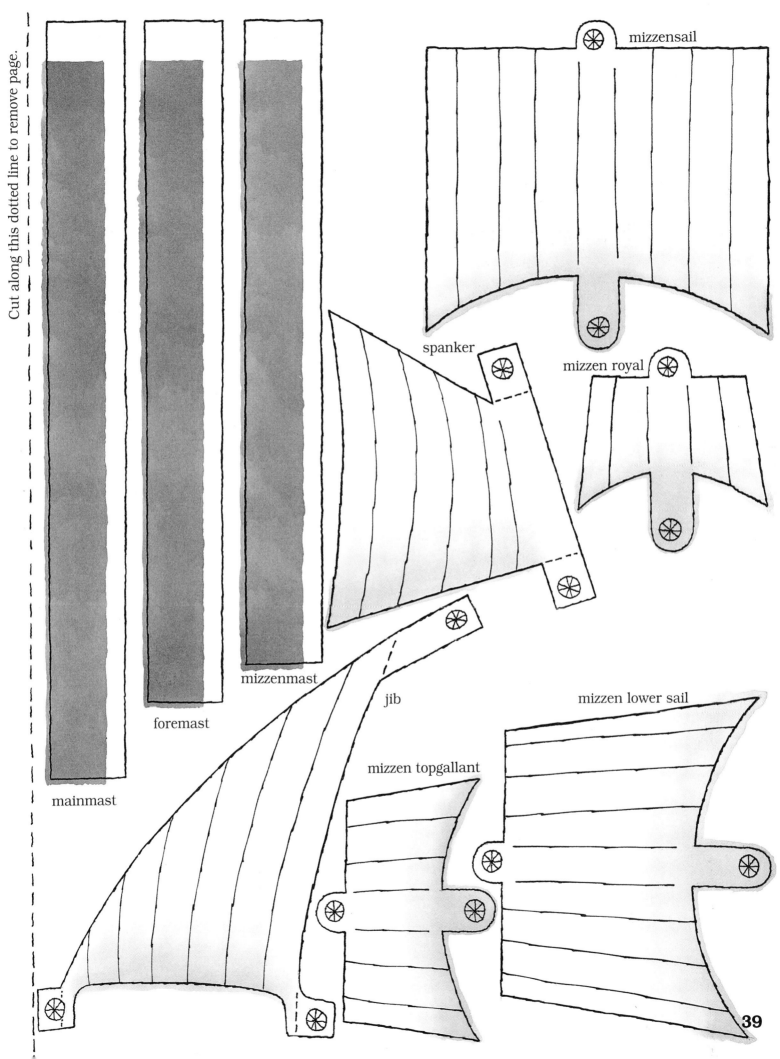

mizzensail

spanker

mizzen royal

mainmast

foremast

mizzenmast

jib

mizzen lower sail

mizzen topgallant

39

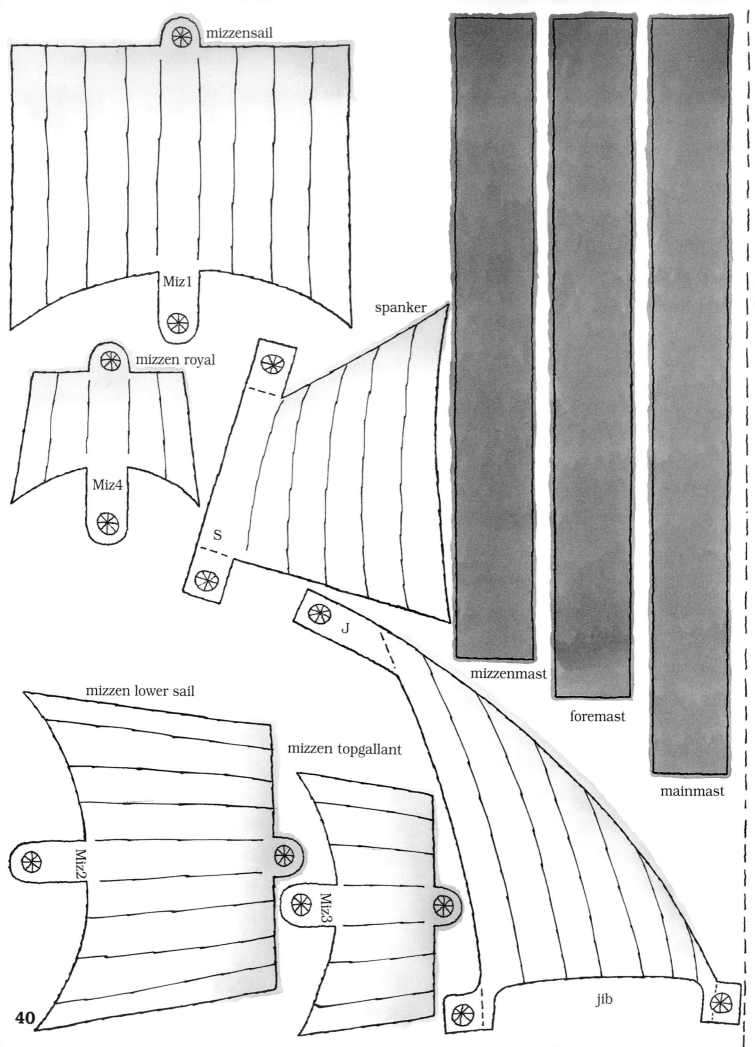

mizzensail

Miz1

mizzen royal

Miz4

spanker

S

J

mizzen lower sail

mizzen topgallant

Miz2

Miz3

mizzenmast

foremast

mainmast

jib

Cut along this dotted line to remove page.

40

superstructure

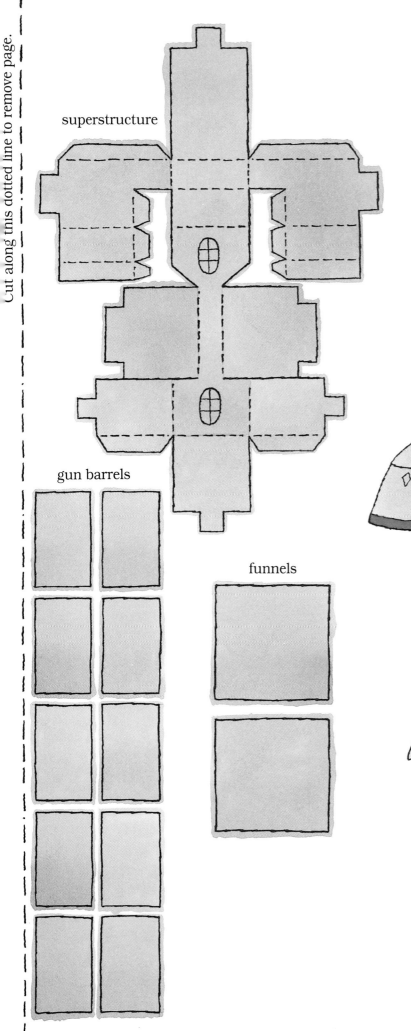

gun barrels

funnels

Dreadnought model

Cut along the solid lines.
Fold along the dotted lines.
See pages 4–5 for assembly instructions.

Glue the hull.

Fold and glue the superstructure.
Glue to hull.

Dreadnought model—assembly

Roll and glue the funnels, gun barrels, and flag pole.
Glue the funnels to superstructure.

Glue the flag to pole and pole to hull.

Glue barrels to the turrets.

Fit the gun turrets to the hull with paper fasteners, matching the numbers for placement.

Paper fasteners allow turrets to turn.

superstructure

gun barrels

funnels

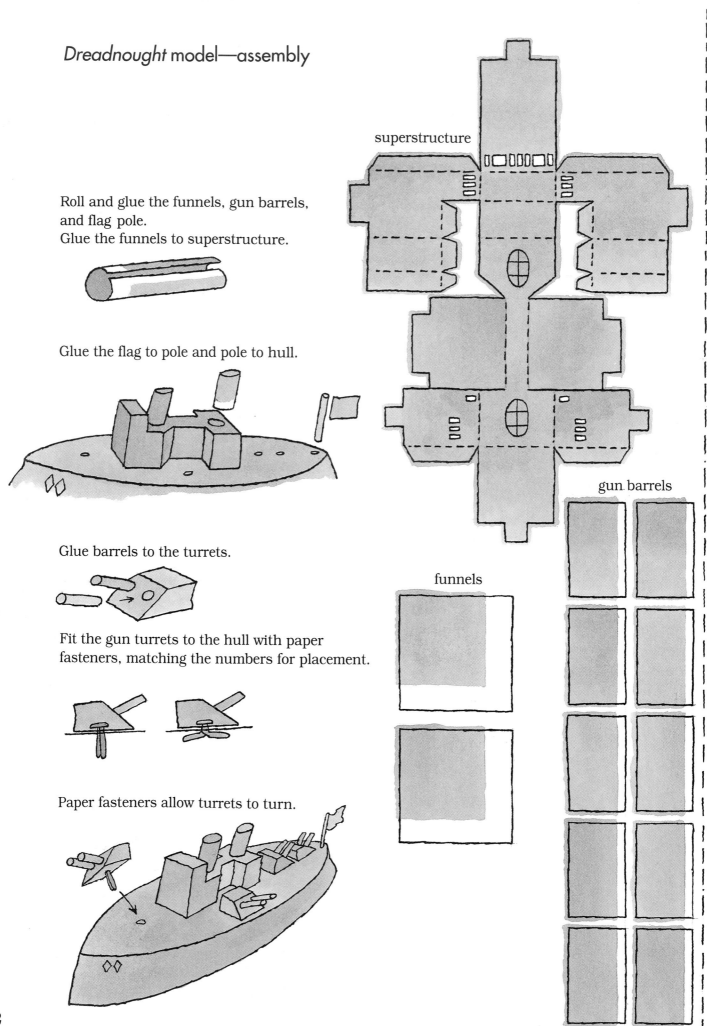

42

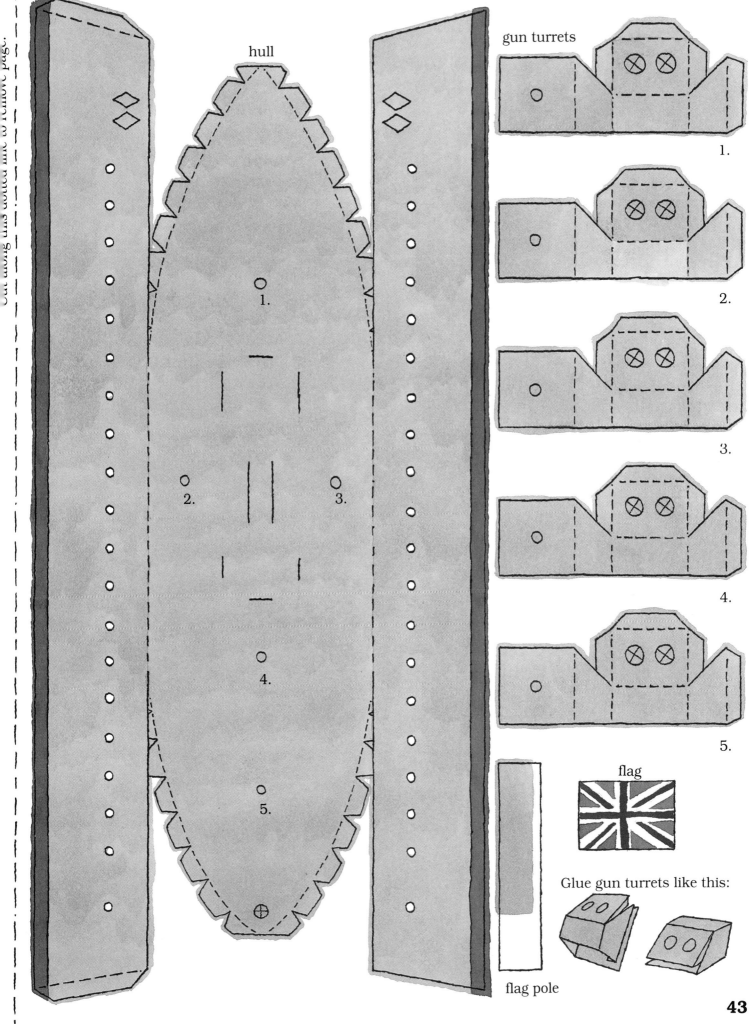

hull

gun turrets

1.

2.

3.

4.

5.

flag

flag pole

Glue gun turrets like this:

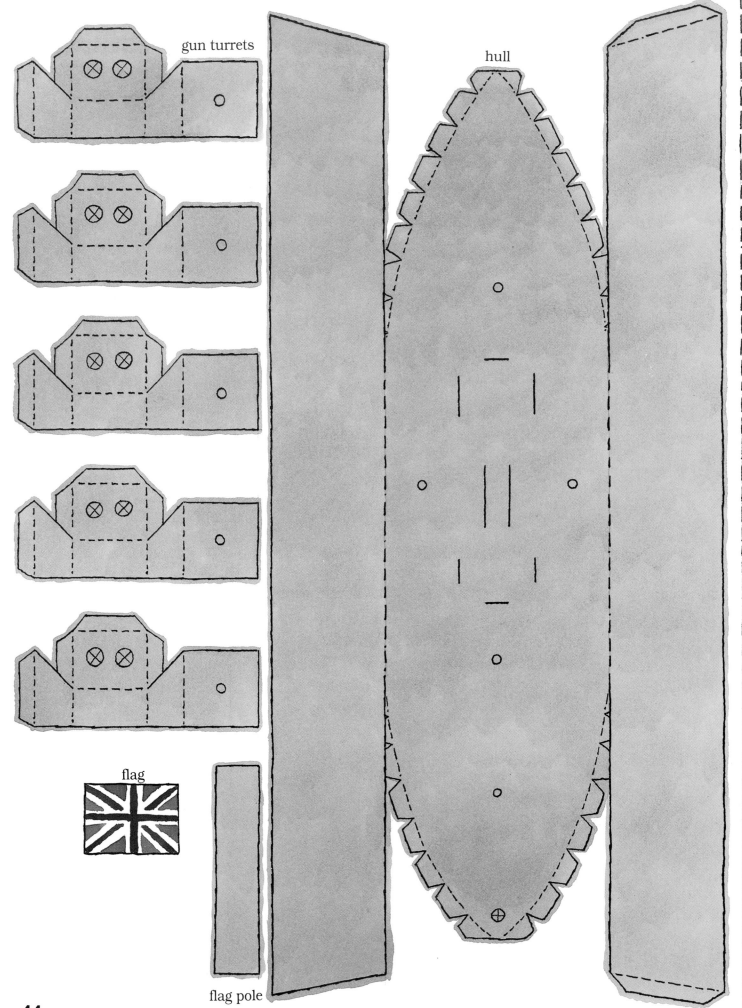

gun turrets

hull

flag

flag pole

The First All-Big-Gun Battleship— The *Dreadnought*

Cannons and guns mounted on ships changed war at sea. By the beginning of the 20th century, battles were being fought by armor-plated steamships, bristling with many different kinds of guns. Big guns that fired at long range from a fast ship were a great advantage in a sea battle.

In 1903 an Italian designer, Vittorio Cuniberti, published plans for "An Ideal Battleship for the British Navy." The British First Sea Lord, Admiral Sir John Fisher, liked the idea, and the ship was designed and built in record time. It was launched in 1906 and named the *Dreadnought*. She was the first of the all-big-gun battleships—with five big guns mounted on revolving turrets—and the first big battleship to have a steam turbine engine. The *Dreadnought* was fast and agile, and, with her accurate guns, she could easily beat any other battleship then afloat.

She was so good that the navies of the world had to scrap their old-fashioned fleets and build new ships! The term *Dreadnought* was later used to describe any "all-big-gun battleship."

The First Nuclear Submarine – The *Nautilus*

The United States, Russia, Britain, and France all use nuclear submarines for defense. A nuclear submarine armed with missiles can stay hidden deep under the sea for months. And an enemy might think twice about attacking if he does not know from *where* the counterattack will come.

The U.S. launched the first nuclear-powered submarine in January, 1954. It was named the *Nautilus* after a famous submarine from World War II, and the original fictional submarine from Jules Verne's adventure story, *Twenty Thousand Leagues under the Sea*. She was actually a steamship, because the nuclear reactor made steam to drive a steam turbine engine.

As the first successful submarine engine that didn't need oxygen, the *Nautilus* could stay under water much longer than earlier submarines. In 1958 the *Nautilus* became the first ship to travel beneath the North Pole. She was clumsy and slow, but she led the way for more nuclear submarines to be built.

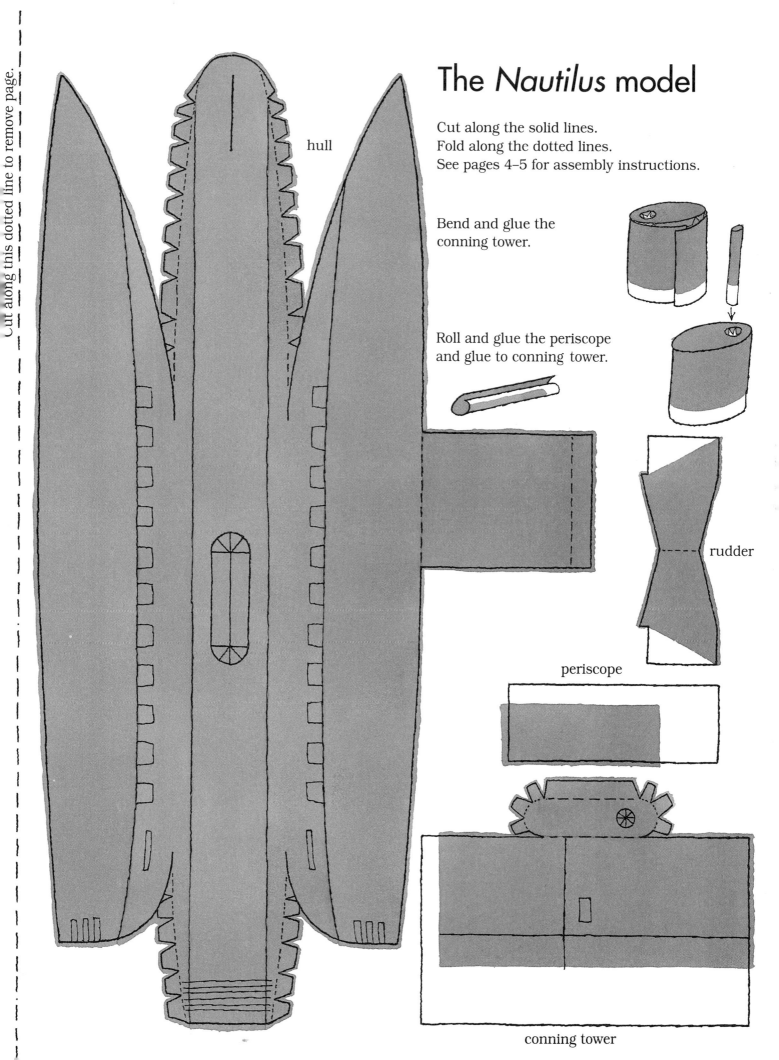

hull

The *Nautilus* model

Cut along the solid lines.
Fold along the dotted lines.
See pages 4–5 for assembly instructions.

Bend and glue the
conning tower.

Roll and glue the periscope
and glue to conning tower.

rudder

periscope

conning tower

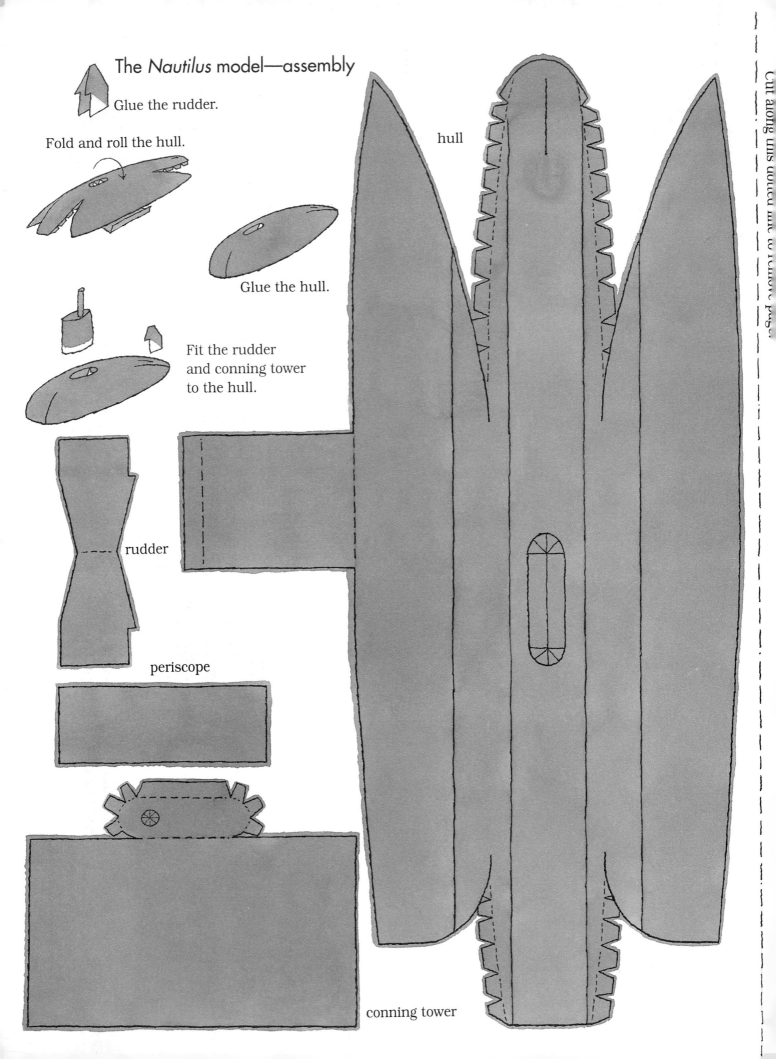

The *Nautilus* model—assembly

Glue the rudder.

Fold and roll the hull.

Glue the hull.

Fit the rudder and conning tower to the hull.

rudder

periscope

hull

conning tower